CREATIVE WARFARE

LESSONS OF THE CONQUEST

Published by The Conquest Project. A division of The Dark Titan Company.

This book is meant for educational purposes such as creativity, planning, and strategy.

Paperback ISBN: 979-8-9899434-6-3
eBook ISBN: 979-8-9899434-7-0

theconquestproject.com

CREATIVE WARFARE

LESSONS OF THE CONQUEST

TY'RON W. C. ROBINSON II

CONTENTS

FOREWORD

This book was written for educational purposes.

Take notes to keep remembrance.

THE CONSTANT STRUGGLE

The constant struggle of the Arts is the main factor of the *Creative Warfare*. Whether be company against company, writer against writer, artist against artist.

The only struggle between them is which will come out on top of the war.

The first battle takes place within the minds of the individuals or groups.

The battle dealing with self-doubt of your craft. Not having the faith in your ability to perform the talent that's been given to you.

Telling yourself to achieve and accept mediocrity while others around you strive to reach for higher goals in order to have their talent and craft be presented before kings rather than men.

You, the creators, have to understand and realize that it is you that will achieve success or failure.

The choices are all in your hands and in the hands of your talent, however you choose to use it.

Because what you decide to do with your talent will have an effect on the masses. You can either inspire them with your work or you can destroy them with it.

Understand that you have power within your grasp. Use it wisely.

Remember, the first battle takes place within the mind.

Your mind is and must be at work whether it's against a physical enemy or yourselves.

Before you enter the war, you have to overcome the battle and that battle starts with you facing yourself.

THE CULTURES THROUGHOUT THE INDUSTRY

As we all know, the cultures change rapidly throughout times and seasons. One culture chooses the old paths while the following cultures chooses individualism and free of choice.

Some cultures will promote being smart and innovative. The other culture will promote being ignorant and docile.

Yet, within those culture changes, the creativity also changes in many and only stays the same in a few, but evolves from thereon.

The cultures are ultimately controlled by forces that many cannot see nor have they ever heard of. Those forces control a mass of wealth and own more corporations than anyone could imagine.

But the twist of that matter is the forces have no creativity and no vision themselves.

They must seek those with the creative power to do their bidding by changing and twisting the culture.

That's what is known today as the Culture Industry.

The Soviets called the actors and directors the Culture Leaders as they were responsible for feeding the masses with new upgrades and new trends in order to keep them afloat in time. Nazi

Germany used the film industry to feed the masses propaganda in order achieve their goals of conquering.

DEVELOPING THE PLANS

You must develop plans in the *Creative Warfare*. Whether the plans mirror military strategies or your own personal planning. In the warfare, you must have a plan.

Be it small or large.

Be it by yourself or with an army at your disposal.

Those plans should include techniques of how to deal with the enemy, their characters, their stories, and their universe.

How can you succeed without a plan that challenges those four obstacles?

You cannot, unless you have a stroke of luck and that is a stroke in itself.

Your plan must be silent and unusual to the enemy and consider the cost of your plans.

Because if they manage to see it, they will have the upper hand on you and will eliminate you from the warfare to where you'll have a harder time making a comeback for yourself and your talent.

THE COMPETITION

The competition may seem fierce to some in the *Creative Warfare*. With others taking the daring opportunities to jump out and stand their ground. Meanwhile, there are those who wait patiently till it's the right time to strike.

The truth is your Competition is not only yourself, but the other Creators.

This is the reality.

The writers and artists across the globe through social media and those that stand in front of you.

Some are your friends, colleagues, associates, whatever they may be, you must remember they are your competition.

Business wise, other companies are your competition. Sure deals are done to develop a partnership between the two or three or four.

But the real truth is each of them are fighting for the minds of the masses day in and day out.

Some will see it as fun and entertaining for people to enjoy. Some will see it as a means to waste time, valuable time.

Few will understand that it isn't just to entertain the masses. It is there to educate them of the world they live and what could be.

YOUR UNIVERSE IS YOUR ARSENAL

Take a look at your universe and by universe I mean the one you have created yourself.

The fictional universe where the characters you have created reside.

The worlds that dwell in your universe, the realms, and the dimensions, the powers, and the rulers that exists within your fictional universe.

Look at it closely.

Some have created their characters just to be in the stories presented to them and after the stories are out in the public eye, they vanish into the unknown of the fictional universe and fall into what is known as the *Public Domain*.

Some chose to create characters for the sake of pure fun and pleasure, to where their characters only appear on certain occasions and disappear into the wind, being swept away.

Few have taken the lengthy time and study to come up with the idea to plan out the lives of their characters from their birth to their death. They have planned the beginning of their fictional universe and even planned its end.

The amount of your universe's characters, worlds, realms, and stories will have an impact upon your enemies in the warfare. They will present themselves a force that only your enemies and opposing forces will see.

The richness that your universe will possess will be unlike any the opposing forces have seen before.

Truthfully, they must have a fear for your universe and the power that comes with it.

That fear will bring the curiosity of the masses to your universe and to your stories.

Where does your universe fit among these categories. You have to know because your universe will become your arsenal in the *Creative Warfare.*

The war isn't won by the writers and artists throwing pen and paper at one another across desks and tables. It's won by the characters and stories they have created to achieve their purpose.

WAGING WAR

The war itself deals with the characters and stories brought out by its creators. Whether they're brought out into the field with only words or with only pictures.

Some will mix the words with pictures, using the prose-illustrated method to suit their plans.

The war will present itself before in all the forms of media and storytelling.

The battles that your characters and worlds are facing will also be at war with the competition's.

You could be walking down an aisle in a store and your enemy have placed an attack on you.

You could be in an airport and your enemy has a showcase presenting itself before your takeoff flight.

You could be in a theater and your enemy has placed a trailer that you are about to witness.

Always consider the cost of your arsenal before heading out to the battlefield to confront the opposing force.

It will be up to you when you'll have to invade the competition
and eventually conquer them and their possessions, what's known
as their IP (*Intellectual Property*). Conquering is another term for
acquiring.

Waging the war will take the methods you have presented before
yourself before engaging in the war.

The plans you have developed and the studying of your
competition.

All will be revealed and settled while engaging in the war.

TACTICAL SITUATIONS

Discovering the tactics that can be used in the *Creative Warfare* are not far out of place. The tactics start with the plans you have created and intend to use in the warfare.

The tactics also include advertising, marketing, and licensing.

Using it in creative and innovative ways to improve your work and your creations.

Traditional tactics only help when the situation requires of them to intervene.

Again, you must become innovative in your tactics in order to succeed. How else can you overcome when you'll just going with the status quo.

Throw away the status quo and make your own moves.

Your tactics should include how your work influences the masses.

Does it entertain them?

Does it teach them?

Does it keep them dumb and docile?

Keep a limit onto yourself in order to avoid using all of your techniques against one before you find yourself with no techniques against an army of creators.

SPIRITUAL AND CREATIVE ENERGY

The energy that will drive you from the battle to the war is both spiritual and creative.

The spiritual energy should feed the creative energy.

As Leonardo Da Vinci had said himself, *"Where the Spirit does not work with the hand, there is no art."*

Be it mediation or prayer with fasting, you must refill your spiritual energy and continue to keep it full at all times.

We all have our moments of fault and low, but it is up to us to overcome and endure the times so we can keep reaching higher and achieve what we've come to collect.

That energy should increase your talent and should aid you in being successful in the warfare.

STRENGTHS AND WEAKNESSES

Simple than what other perceive. You present your strengths and you hide your weaknesses.

Do not allow others to see your weaknesses in full detail.

Otherwise, they'll know what to do in order to succeed above you.

Your strengths must be present in all your works.

Your works should showcase your strengths of your talent and creativity.

It should have the power to inspire others or instill them with fear.

Whether it be for good or bad.

When you spot your competition's weaknesses, use it to an advantage for the gain of your universe.

When you see their strengths, give respect and honor.

Because with respect and honor comes full trust between opposing creators.

GENERALS AND SOLDIERS

The generals in this warfare are the creators.

Business wise, it is the CEO or founder of the company and the soldiers the employees of the company.

Occasionally the soldiers would be others within the group.

The ones that do little to mid work.

Individually, the creator is the general and the characters are the soldiers.

Doing battle in a variety of sorts.

From movies to TV to books to video games to plays to merchandise.

Your soldiers must be at work just as you, the general, are at work.

The soldiers you conquer and recruit in latter times must conform to your order of things or they will be a stumbling block on your creative energies, your planning, and your arsenal.

ALWAYS ON THE WATCH

Mind your own business should be the first thing on your mind within the *Creative Warfare*.

There are times when you must take a glimpse at your opposing creators and see what they have come up with and what they are possibly planning in the process of time.

It will show you what you can do and what you shouldn't do before its appointed time.

Take the right time to burn the midnight oil and make yourself a watch period, a small one, in order to have the knowledge needed and an advantage planted.

THE UNIFORMED IN THE WARFARE

Writers and artists that are unaware of this warfare taking place have a choice to make and it concerns their entire career in the Arts.

They can either open their ears and learn about the *Creative Warfare* and become proactive in it or they can hear and not take a single chance of doing anything in the warfare besides watching, which will not grant you success in the war.

Lastly, they can neither see or hear and become nothing more than creators who continually struggle to make a way into the Arts and end up failing to achieve their place as creators.

The choice is ultimately up to them and them alone.

YOUR CHIEF END IN THE WARFARE

What is your chief end in the warfare?

Is it to gain the fame and fortune of the Arts? To be a star amongst the people? Signing countless autographs and taking pictures with people you don't even know?

Is your chief end to boast in yourself and in your works?

Is your chief end to boast in a Higher Power than yourself that gave you the talent necessary to achieve success in the Arts.

Your chief end in the warfare will determine what you've come to achieve and what you've come to do in this warfare.

This is the *Creative Warfare*.

Keep your mind open and your ideas flowing.

Remember, *Ecclesiastes 3:8* mentions, there's a time of peace and there's a time of war.

METHODS OF THE CONQUEST
FOUR KEY FACTORS OF THE CREATIVE WARFARE

CREATIVE WARFARE #1: THE CONSTANT STRUGGLE
- The choices are in your HANDS
- You can either INSPIRE or DESTROY
- Understand that you have the POTENTIAL
- Remember the first battle takes place WITHIN

CREATIVE WARFARE #2: THE CULTURE INDUSTRY
- Seek for the OLD PATHS
- Promote INNOVATION over IGNORANCE
- Creativity is your WEAPON
- You can CHANGE the culture

CREATIVE WARFARE #3: DEVELOPING THE PLANS
- Be it SMALL or LARGE
- SUCCESS depends on it
- Focus on your TECHNIQUES
- Your PLANS must be SILENT

CREATIVE WARFARE #4: THE COMPETITION
- CALCULATE your strategies
- Choose your COMPETITION
- VALUE your TIME
- EDUCATE, ENLIGHTEN, and ENTERTAIN

CREATIVE WARFARE #5: YOUR UNIVERSE IS YOUR ARSENAL

- CREATE your CHARACTERS and WORLDS
- Craft your STORIES to INSPIRE
- Strategize your WORLDBUILDING skills
- Have FUN and ENJOY your CREATIONS

CREATIVE WARFARE #6: WAGING WAR

- Consider the COSTS
- CONQUER, then ACQUIRE
- DEVELOP your PLANS
- ENGAGE in the WARFARE

CREATIVE WARFARE #7: TACTICAL SITUATIONS

- Tactics begin with your PLANS
- Use CREATIVE and INNOVATIVE ways
- Throw away the STATUS QUO
- Keep a LIMIT on YOURSELF

CREATIVE WARFARE #8: SPIRITUAL AND CREATIVE ENERGY

- REFILL your SPIRITUALITY
- INCREASE your CREATIVITY
- MEDITATION and FASTING
- OVERCOME and ENDURE

CREATIVE WARFARE #9: STRENGTHS AND WEAKNESSES

- Your STRENGTHS must be PRESENT
- Showcase your TALENT and CREATIVITY
- INSPIRE others or INSTILL fear
- Have RESPECT and HONOR

CREATIVE WARFARE #10: GENERALS AND SOLDIERS

- CREATORS are the GENERALS
- CHARACTERS are the SOLDIERS
- CONQUER and RECRUIT
- Always do the WORK

CREATIVE WARFARE #11: ALWAYS ON THE WATCH

- MIND your own BUSINESS
- OBSERVE when necessary
- PLOT accordingly
- BURN the MIDNIGHT OIL

CREATIVE WARFARE #12: THE UNIFORMED IN THE WARFARE

- WRITERS and ARTISTS must make a CHOICE
- OPEN your EARS, LISTEN CLOSELY
- Take ACTION
- The CHOICE is YOURS ALONE

CREATIVE WARFARE #13: YOUR CHIEF END IN THE WARFARE

- What is YOUR CHIEF END?
- Your CHIEF END will determine EVERYTHING
- Keep your MIND open and your IDEAS flowing
- This is the CREATIVE WARFARE

TENETS OF THE CREATIVE WARFARE

1. Understand that you have the power within your grasp. Use it wisely
2. Traditional tactics only help when the situation requires of them to intervene
3. CREATE. ACHIEVE. CONQUER.
4. Conquest is Necessary
5. Your strengths must be present in all your works
6. What you decide to do with your talent will have an effect on the world
7. Promote innovation over ignorance
8. Mind your own business
9. The war is won by the characters and stories you create
10. Consider the Cost
11. Inspire or Destroy
12. The potential is yours to obtain
13. Value your Time
14. Your plans must be silent
15. Take the time to study
16. Build the next generation and beyond
17. Respect and Honor
18. Keep a limit on yourself
19. Engage in the Warfare
20. Strategize your worldbuilding skills.

ABOUT THE AUTHOR

Ty'Ron W. C. Robinson II is the owner of The Dark Titan Company and the creator of The Conquest Project.

FOLLOW THE CONQUEST PROJECT

X/Twitter: @TheProConquest

Instagram: @theconquestproject

Facebook: @theconquestproject

Threads: @theconquestproject

YouTube: @theconquestproject

TikTok: @theconquestproject